WHISKEY

in a

TEACUP

r. k. f.

Her aura is made of whiskey and poetry….
…welcome to her tea party….

She's Hepburn with a twist
A lady like mix
Of badass and class
An ineffable rebel for kicks

Meet me at the corner of morning,
Where the sun and the moon trade shifts
When soft light floods the horizon
With grace and promise as gifts

Kiss me
Taste me like whiskey
Savor my essence, my mind
Ignite the fire…send shivers down my spine

Come here
Let me be your mirror
To reflect to you all that you have given me
Grace, courage and a place to feel free

Kiss your dreams into the hollow of my neck and
your secrets in the crevice of my thighs….
Touch me like we have nothing but time
on our hands, and lust on our minds

Spoon your whiskey into my tea
Strong and slow, stir through me

Sometimes the only thing that will soothe my ache
is the rough of your hand on the smooth of my hip

She'll always be an adventure seeker
your sexual healer
coveting your body like a born again believer....

Rules of a lady in the bedroom:
Wear the lingerie of your skin with the aura of a goddess
While granting yourself permission to finish
Know how to fuck, yet make love like a savant
Seek what you need, then ask for what you want

<u>To Do:</u>
Walk slowly
Savor Happenstance
Seek Delight

She's a lioness with hummingbird dreams

Her magic liked to dance with his logic in the moonlight

Remember who you are my darling,
You are the daughter of the sun and a child of the moon
Your light is both beautiful and necessary

He's her vintage books and moonlight on the sea;
She's his exotic dreams and whiskey laced tea

If you want to understand her soul; study the
words that move her, explore the wild of her
mind, decipher the sound of her silence.

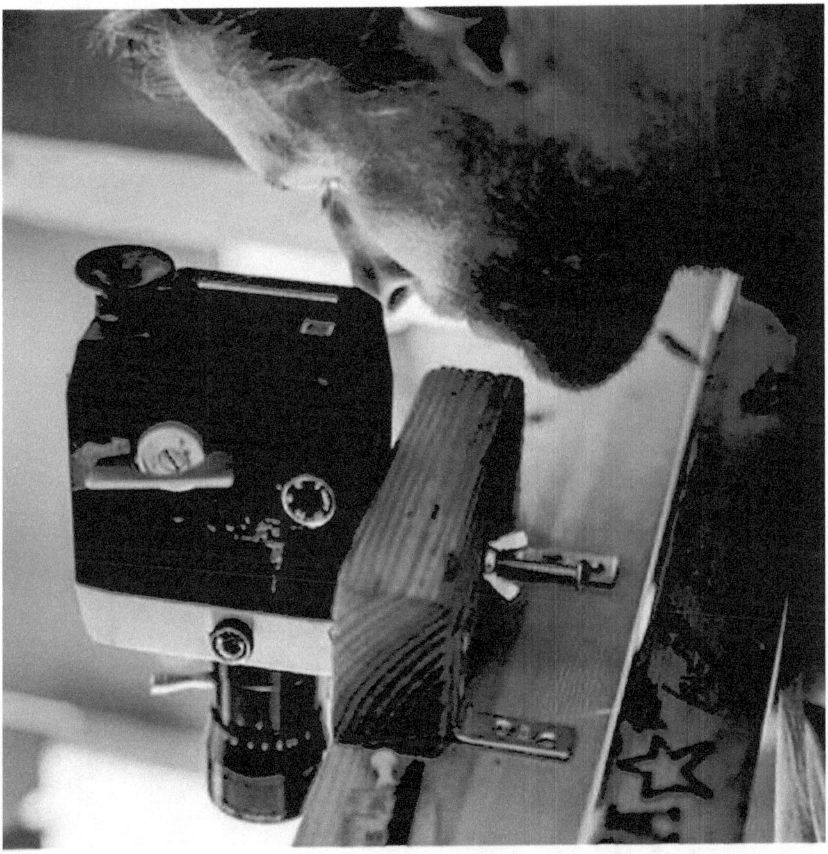

My soul is woven from the essence of
those who have crossed my path…

Legend has it ,
whiskey pixies dance
on the wings of graceful fuckery

Thank you for teaching me how to feel with my eyes closed
When I needed to see the light

This letter is for you:
The you, that likes books and tattoos, bacon and
haikus, combat boots and high heeled shoes…
you have permission to be more than one you.

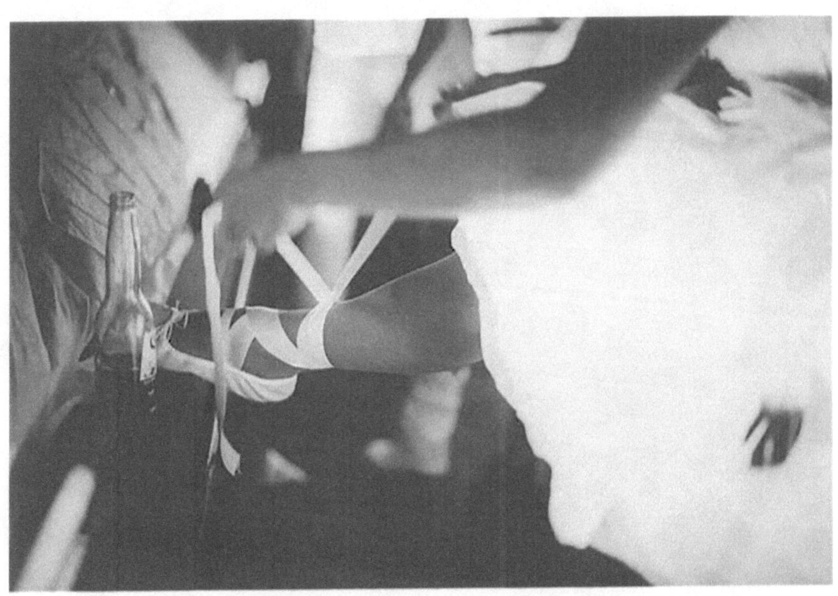

Slow down…
Listen to the soft whispers
Urging you to go on…and let go

As you sift through the moments of your life,
keep only those that make you grow;
with a grateful hand, sweep the others aside.

Could you hear it?
Somewhere in time my soul whispered your name
Those are the days strength appears
in the semblance of softness

From some other time
Some other place
Worlds apart
I've felt your grace
… ever since then,
my heart has been fond of your heart

I would very much like to be a reflection
Of all the unique and intricate parts
of you that bring you peace
…maybe then you would see your worth

The best way to show them who you are darling,
Is to show them who you're not

She said, I am a woman
Lips and hips dipped in honey
Mind and soul soaked in whiskey
….don't fuck with me

Take me on an adventure
Away from this world
I want to get lost in the wild with you

When you go,
My love goes with you
it stands within your shadow
So you are never alone

Bed sheet clasp
Heart beat fast
Breathe abated
Lust sedated

Come, write your poetry on my body
Graffiti me with erotic artistry

There's a window of time
Silently exposing
Forever closing
The space between you and I

Time, a healer and a thief

Celebrate your body when you're young
Appreciate its worth as you get older
Grace and Beauty are sisters
Harmonious in the eye of the beholder

She said,
All I want, all I ask, from what I sense
Is a life of prayer, work, laughter and silence

Thank you for taking what you wanted
and then walking away
You made me realize that I was the most
worthy thing you left behind

    Whiskey in a Teacup

Regret is a nasty bitch
She steals the moments
You once wanted
Then makes your mind her slave
…don't let her in

All is fair in love and war
Yet not the unrequited score
This debt transcends all of time
This I know – I've paid for mine

Whisper hallelujah to the shadows
Then listen for the light,
Your grace is your resilience
Within the dark of night

Overthinking withers the mind and weakens the spirit

I wish you warmth when the world would prefer
you to be cold. I wish you success to overbalance
hardship. I wish you humor that plants a twinkle
in your eye. I wish you happiness to overshadow
grief. But above all, I wish you peace.